Tear g

Janis Grun

"We do briefing on a monthly basis from the top to the bottom of the organisation. It costs about £1m for the privilege but it is certainly worth it. I commend it to you."

George Turnbull
Chairman and Managing Director, Talbot Motors.

First published October 1983 by
The Industrial Society
Peter Runge House
3 Carlton House Terrace
London SW1Y 5DG
Telephone 01-839 4300

Reprinted April 1984
Reprinted November 1984
Reprinted January 1985
Reprinted March 1985
Reprinted September 1985
Reprinted February 1987
Reprinted January 1988

ISBN 0 85290 300 6

Many thanks to *The Guardian*
for cover photographs

Contemprint Limited, London SE1

Contents

Foreword

Team Briefing is the basis of true employee involvement at work. It enables management to *know* that all employees are receiving information about the organisation and their own teams' performance through their immediate team leaders.

As of 1983, the Employment Act requires companies to make a statement of their communication and involvement policy in their shareholders report. Many companies will be able to say they are using Team Briefing among other forms of communication and involvement.

In the last two years The Industrial Society has helped more than 200 organisations to install Team Briefing in both the public and private sector and has been instrumental in the training of over 6,000 managers and supervisors in the skills of briefing their teams. This book has been written in order to pull together the knowledge gained from this experience from the many organisations that we have worked with in the area of communication for over 20 years.

DAVID FELDMAN
Division Director

1 What is Team Briefing?

Objective

Team Briefing is a system of communication operated by line management. Its objective is to make sure that *all* employees know and understand what they and others in the company are doing and why. It is a management information system. It is based on leaders and their teams getting together in groups for half an hour on a regular basis to talk about things that are relevant to their work.

History

This is not a new piece of management theory of course. The Roman Army used briefing in small teams, which was apparently one of their great secrets of success during battle! In more recent times, many industrial companies introduced Briefing Groups ten or even twenty years ago. Many of these systems, however, were used as 'cascade' systems which merely passed information from 'top' to 'bottom' of the company. This was quite exciting for the first few months while there was quite a lot of 'new' information, but once the novelty 'had worn off' employees often 'switched off' and boards of directors spent hours trying to make up messages of encouragement and interest for their employees. Companies that had made briefing successful were always those who introduced a vital element—local information.

Team Briefing today

The most important feature of Team Briefing, as the name implies—is the team. Naturally, there is also a 'cascade' element in Team Briefing—the system is structured so that information can be added in at higher levels—but each briefer at whatever level of the organisation writes their own brief before other information is passed down to them. A different emphasis from Briefing Groups.

Putting it into context

Briefing the team is part of a manager's job—a Team Briefing System merely formalises something that good managers and supervisors do anyway. It is not a panacea. It will not improve all a company's communication overnight. There are many ways of communicating information—this is one of them. It does not replace existing methods, it complements them. However, if your organisation does not brief information regularly through work group leaders to their teams—you are missing the crucial basis for good management communication.

If management communication in your organisation is compared to a car, Team Briefing is like the engine. Lots of other parts make up the car, without which the engine would be no good, but without the engine, the body and wheels are mere decoration—it is the engine that makes it go. *Team Briefing* is based on the most practical and effective method known of communicating through the manager to all employees.

2 What are the benefits?

Team Briefing is not a welfare exercise. It makes the organisation more efficient. Of course employees appreciate being kept in the picture and may be happier as well. The main benefits, however, are more practical and work related.

It reinforces management
"He who communicates is he who leads"—an old saying, but true. The very act of getting the team together and talking means that *the manager is seen to be the leader*. This is particularly important for first line supervision. Over the years the poor supervisor has all too often been forgotten as part of the management team, and not suprisingly, ceases to behave like one. Team Briefing makes them manage again because it clearly differentiates them from their people and reminds them and their team that they are accountable for the group's performance. In some companies, supervisors say that it is the first time that they have been told information through the management line, rather than having to go to the Shop Steward for it! Team Briefing gives management credibility, and makes sure that employees hear management information from management.

> ***Example:***
> A young supervisor on the shop floor of a company in the West Country was reticent when told to brief. When asked why she didn't want to, she said that it wasn't part of the job—that was what management was there to do. When asked what she thought made her different from the other girls on her line she said—"more money". After briefing, she began to realise that she also had more responsibility because it wasn't until she talked to the team that she saw her effect on the team and her responsibility for getting them to achieve results. She no longer thinks that "more money" is the main difference between her and others.

It increases commitment
Team Briefing improves people's commitment to the task that their team is involved in and also to the wider 'team' of the company or organisation as a whole. People need to know how they are doing as a team and be told whether they are meeting targets or not. It is extremely difficult to be committed to something when you do not know what it is. Talking to people regularly about how we are doing and whether we are overcoming the problems gives people an objective to work for. It will not make a boring job interesting—but it will give work a purpose, and give people a direction. Explaining 'why' something needs to be done is as important as

telling them 'what' has to be done. Even if people do not agree with something they can accept it if they understand the reason for it.

Example:
At a cosmetic factory the Japanese lines had to produce 100% quality—when the European lines had to produce a far lower standard. The workers on the Japanese lines were reluctant, because although they knew what they had to achieve, they didn't know why it was any different from the other lines. It was explained through Team Briefing that the European market did not demand 100% but the Japanese did. Not only that—but they checked all the cases arriving and if they were to find one bottle imperfect, it would all be shipped back to England at the company's cost—a very expensive business! Everyone in the factory is aware of the Japanese quality problem now, and although nobody likes the situation, the quality level is improving all the time and the company is aiming for a 100% quality standard and is very nearly there.

Other areas where increased commitment has resulted from explanation and regular reminders are: absenteeism, wastage, better productivity, greater awareness of safety and good housekeeping, cost savings.

Example:
An Assurance Company found that it was spending enormous amounts on telephone calls. There was a drive spearheaded by the briefing system to combat this. Every month people were told how much the telephone bill had cost, and reminded of the need to save costs. After six months of this, the company's telephone bill had dropped by 25%. Afterwards, it was briefed occasionally to remind people so that they did not slip back into bad habits.

Commitment to the team is vital, if the individual is to contribute effectively to it. But it is also important for each person to appreciate that everyone belongs to a wider 'team' of the company. It is very hard for an individual on a lathe to identify himself with an engineering company employing 600 people! However, it is important for him to realise that his work is part of a whole effort; he needs to know what the company's objective is at the end of the day.

Example:
I once walked the floor in an Engineering Company. In the assembly shop, the foreman told me that the company's worst problem was deliveries. "We never meet any delivery dates!" According to George—it was not his section's fault, but the machine room who never got the parts to them in time. I asked the machine room foreman why his parts were always late. It appeared that it was not his fault either—it was stores—poor stock control—the stuff was never there. Naturally the stores blamed planning (everyone does in the end) and I

failed to find anyone in the whole company who thought that it was *their* problem—it was always someone else's. Funny isn't it that people could not see that if deliveries continued to be late—orders would go elsewhere and it would not matter whose fault it was in the end! Perhaps no-one had ever reminded people of the company's objectives.

It prevents misunderstandings

In many companies, the left hand does not seem to know what the right hand is doing. Misunderstandings can be costly, time consuming and occasionally embarassing. Often in management, we assume that people know a lot more than they do. One of the things we assume is that people know who people are.

Example:

I recently ran a course for a group of managers and supervisors; the Managing Director introduced me (but not himself) and people were looking a bit confused. When he left the room, they asked me who he was!

This example is funny but potentially embarassing. However, some misunderstandings are costly. In a very large company (over 1,000 people on one site) the Finance Director changed the procedure for signing invoices. The trouble was, that he did not communicate this to anyone other than the management team by memo. Lower down the organisation people were frustrated for days because they no longer knew what the system was and spent hours going from person to person trying to find someone who knew (or thought they knew!). A great deal of time was wasted, morale dropped very sharply, and the Finance Director's popularity hit rock bottom! It would have been simple to brief this information.

It helps to accept change

Human beings dislike change—with the few exceptions of people who thrive on it—most people are insecure when faced with something that they are nor used to. It is important, therefore, to give people the longest time possible to understand why change will not necessarily make people like it or even agree with it—but will help them to accept it.

Example:

Normal sane people have been known to turn into nervous wrecks during a move from one building to another for instance. Desks would disappear overnight, and if you left the building for more than a few days, you found that you had been allocated a broom cupboard for an office as all the larger rooms had been taken. On the day of the move, so few people had any idea of what the 'plan' was that half of the filing system was lost in the ensuing chaos. No wonder no-one wanted to move, despite the fact that the new building was newer and better. Most seriously, workforces have actually been known to take strike action over moves between buildings—more often than not, this has happened where management have successfully communicated with management—but not checked that the key people, the supervisors, have been told and in turn have told their people.

Other changes such as re-structuring and redundancies will cause severe problems if people have not been given enough information to be able to understand the reason for change and accept it.

Example:
In a famous car company where redundancies were announced, one of the workers was asked by a reporter at the gates if they were going to fight it. "No," he replied. "The management have been telling us about the problems and our financial situation for over a year now—they could not do anything else if we're going to save the company." Of course, the company concerned had been talking to the workforce about company performance for years—companies that start to tell people how badly they are doing just before redundancies are announced, or more commonly, just before negotiation, lose a lot of credibility—they are seen to be manipulating rather than being open. Credibility relies on regularity over a period of time; Team Briefing provides this.

It helps control the grapevine
Most organisations have not got grapevines—they have whole vineyards! Regular Team Briefing definitely helps to control the grapevine and will reduce a vineyard to a mere grapevine—but it is unlikely to get rid of it. Neither will it necessarily be faster than the grapevine, which is the fastest method of organisational communication known to man. It often gets the facts right as well—but it is destructive and can strangle morale unless it is controlled. A useful definition of the grapevine is "the passing on of information by people who cannot be held accountable for it." If people cannot be held accountable—any amount of 'slanting' can take place *en route.* The 'slanting' is nearly always to the disadvantage of management.

Example:
"George has been offered the job of manager in the Commercial Department" (this is true). ". . . and you know why he got it, don't you?" He ("Plays golf with the Chairman"/"sleeps with the Director's Secretary"/"went to the same school as . . .", etc—this is the fruits of the grapevine).

The grapevine denigrates management and lowers morale.

> ***Example:***
> A severe case occured in a finance company that was clearly in trouble and where staff knew that there was a possibility that they might be sold. One morning the office was buzzing about three men who had arrived first thing and had made an offer to buy them. There had been three men in reception early that morning—but they were from British Telecom and were not buying the company. They were fixing the telephones! Very little work was done that morning as you might imagine.

If there is a regular briefing system, people will still listen to the grapevine but will wait to hear the 'official' version from their manager. The manager will be better informed through the regular briefing meetings and so is more likely to know the answer than he would have been previously. If he does not know the answer, the briefings will have opened a channel through which he can find out the answer.

It improves upward communication
Senior managers find it difficult to understand why people do not seem to have good ideas or even views about what is happening. Why does the Consultative Committee always discuss the chips in the canteen—or worse still—the dreaded coffee machine? Why has no-one put anything other than obscene suggestions in the company Suggestion Box? Involvement does not seem to be as easy as it sounds—people are not rushing forward to contribute—but why? Lack of information and understanding is often at the root. If people do not know what the main problems are and if they are not clear about what needs to be achieved, it is like trying to think without brain cells. If people can relate a problem to their own jobs, then they can have ideas or views about it to voice themselves or to pass to the representative (who has long since stopped asking for people's views because they had none!). But to ask people for ideas and views when they are living in an information vacuum is clearly silly. Team Briefing meetings should not be used for consultation or problem solving—mixing two objectives merely confuses the issue. But feedback as a result of these meetings is a common side benefit and if harnessed, can revitalise or kindle the upward communication channel.

> ***Example:***
> At a cosmetic manufacturers, after management had briefed the need for 100% quality on the Japanese line, it was a supervisor who came up with the idea for a simple filter to go on the end of the machine, which would prevent foreign bodies going into the cream. Once people realised the need for higher quality, they began to see ways of achieving it as they were working.

3 Objections to starting Team Briefing

Team Briefing is based on common sense and good management practice. However, there are a number of objections that can arise before an organisation 'takes the plunge' and I have listed the ones that seem to arise most often.

"We all do this already"

This objection is normally voiced by a member of senior management. Senior management often communicates regularly, for instance, most companies have a monthly board and/or executive meeting. Often the directors have monthly meetings with their managers—but rarely does this continue down the line to the shop floor or the office floor. Unless there is a system that can be monitored with the information passed on by someone who can be held accountable for it, communication normally does not cross the 'supervisor barrier'. One of the good things about this system is that senior managers know that people are told. Are you *sure* that people know?

It is unlikely that *all* managers and supervisors do it already. There are always those who do not like to communicate, those who think that knowledge is power; those who always have other priorities and are so busy that they never really get round to it. A system makes sure that *everyone* briefs—not just those who would do it anyway. In the final analysis, if you really do . . . "all do this already"—you are Team Briefing of your own accord, but read on to see whether you *really* do.

"They already know everything"

This is a favourite cry of the Finance Director or the Accounts Manager, "They see all the information about the company in their jobs anyway". It is always interesting to talk privately to the people in their departments—who invariably say "he never tells us anything—he dosen't believe in communicating". These people may have a mass of figures and facts, but they often have not got the time to sit and consider the implications of them, or what it means to the company. The pieces of information are the individual pieces of a jigsaw puzzle. During the course of their work they must indeed see the entire picture—but it is fragmented. Someone needs to fit the pieces together so that it can be appreciated.

Strangely it is more likely to be office managers and heads of white collar departments who will believe this statement rather than people in charge of blue-collar workers. In fact, information is often thought to be one of the big differences between the two, Hence, I often hear managers say "It's not like the factory up here you know—I can see why *they* need Team Briefing, but in the offices—we all know it anyway". Normally, the speaker is sadly deluded. A simple way to check is to walk around and ask people in non-managerial jobs about topics that you would expect them to know about. Perhaps they do know it already—perhaps they do not.

It will cost too much/take too much time"
This is a valid objection to raise. It will cost money and it will take time. Installing Team Briefing is an act of investing for the future. Initially the time/cost factor is high—but remember that the system, if put in properly, will last forever. So after the first few months, the cost is one of time—half an hour a month for most people and an hour a month for briefers. This lost time will certainly affect production—but not as much as you may think—on a 40-hour-week it works out approximately 0.3% of productive time. Not difficult to make up—unless you are a continuous process, in which case the approach needs to be flexible to prevent enormous losses!

It is important to invest time and money into the system to get it off to a solid start. Do it properly and it will last—if you are planning to do it half heartedly it could do more harm than good. If the system fails, people will list it with all those other management "flavours of the month", that were grasped enthusiastically and then petered out after a few months. Loss of management credibility will be a greater cost than that of setting Team Briefing up properly in the first place. It will be a long time before you can have another go—people will say "we tried Team Briefing and it dosen't work". Employing an 'outsider' to help set it up can be costly, but with a greater knowledge of the pitfalls and solutions to problems that have worked in other organisations and the important advantage of objectivity—an outside adviser can be your greatest help. Apart from this, the other time costs are those of a co-ordinator who sets up and monitors the system (for more information see the chapter on How to Implement) and the cost of all briefers attending training courses (run on site if possible). Be prepared to spend time and money initially. The benefits of the system merit it.

"Our supervisors/foremen couldn't brief"
Most supervisors and foremen can brief adequately after some training to give them confidence and a few tips. Remember, we do not need to make people into after dinner speakers and so we are not trying to teach them effective speaking. Some people will always be better than others at talking to their teams and a few will never be able to do it. Most people, however, will be good enough and that is all we need. It is a great mistake to prejudge people's ability or inability to brief—often managers are amazed to find that the experience of briefing completely changes a supervisor.

> ***Example:***
> While I was reviewing Team Briefing at a factory recently—one of the previously shy and reticent foremen rushed up to me to tell me

about how briefing his team had changed his life! The General Manager confirmed afterwards that this chap had developed an amazing enthusiasm—and was in the process of rearranging the entire work pattern of his team to become more efficient. Needless to say, his enthusiasm had also rubbed off on the team. As an aside, he also told me that he is now a regular speaker for rotary clubs and at weddings! Before he had gained his confidence, he had never thought that he would be able to do anything like speak to a group of people, and had assumed that no one would ever trust him to do it. Now they had expected greater things of him, he had delivered them.

"The union won't let us"

First of all, Team Briefing is a management system for communicating management information and explaining the management message. It does not interefere with the role of the union representative, whose job is to represent the views of the employees to management. It does *not* make unions unnecessary; on the contrary, in many organisations the representatives find it a help to have a well informed workforce—because they are more able to express their view as a result.

Normally, union representatives do not want to be put in a position where they are expected to pass on management's message for them—it is not their job and is often in direct conflict with their role as representatives. Managers can be held accountable for the management message—that is what they are paid for—but shop stewards are not and we cannot hold them accountable.

Unfortunately although most unions are happy about briefing as long as management explains what it is and why they are doing it, sometimes the situation can be more tricky. It is especially difficult in companies where the management have allowed the shop steward to become more powerful than the foreman or supervisor—and in some cases—to do the job of the foreman. Sometimes, the unions feel that the right to any information and especially the passing on of information to their members, is theirs alone. In fairness, this situation exists normally because management has historically abdicated its role. In these cases—change will not come overnight—the persistence of management over a period of time in getting its message down, is the only way to move forward with Team Briefing. Normally, the union will not object unless the company is using briefing to undermine its role. However, where it does object, that should not deter us from making moves in the right direction. A presentation to involve the union in an understanding of Team Briefing at the start and perseverence on the part of management has usually been found to overcome any union objections.

"It's too formal for our informal management style"

It may be too formal if the company is small enough for random informality to work. Once a company starts to get larger than about 50 people, it gets harder and harder to remain informal while also retaining efficiency. The structured base of Team Briefing allows the briefers to be as informal as they wish with the structure and of course it does not prevent people from communicating as informally as they wish on an everyday basis. But in a company as in life, where there is a large social group there have to be rules to make sure that the group does not fall apart. Without rules there would be anarchy and a lack of direction. Freedom needs structuring in other words: Team Briefing is merely a structure which enables us to communicate—it does not determine the *way* in which we do it—only that it happened. Structured informality seems to be a safer bet than informal structuring!

"People will just use it to moan"

The meetings can easily turn into moaning sessions if the briefer allows them to. This is why training is so important. It needs to be made quite clear at the start of Team Briefing that the objective of the meeting is to pass on information and to answer questions about that information. It is not a chance to ask every question or to raise every grievance that you never had a chance to air before. People need to be reminded of the grievance procedure and reminded of the role of their shop steward if there is one. Briefing is not consultation, nor negotiation, nor problem solving—it is simply an information session with the chance to ask questions. There should be other forums and opportunities to pursue these other objectives; allowing them to be confused with Team Briefing leads to loss of control and ineffective 'gripe sessions' instead. In short, people will only use the meeting to moan if they are allowed to.

"After the first few briefs we'll run out of information"

It is virtually impossible to run out of information if Team Briefing is being operated properly. The more common problem tends to be that of cutting down the information to fit into half an hour. If the system relies heavily on 'Top Level' information of course it will 'run out'. There is not always a great deal to say to people on the shop floor which is relevant or necessary. There is always relevant information to talk about at local level. This means that each briefer has to be trained to write his or her own brief and not be used merely as a management 'postbox' to pass on information. The next chapter deals with the content of the brief in more depth.

4 How to implement Team Briefing

Team Briefing is a simple concept. However, simplicity is not easy to attain! Over the years, organisations which have successfully implemented and operated Team Briefing have shown that an investment of time and money initially will bring lasting results. Some companies have attempted to start briefing by simply announcing to the company that there will be monthly meetings and expecting them to happen! There are a number of critical steps involved in implementing briefing successfully:

Commitment

It is essential that the top man or woman is committed to making Team Briefing work, and is involved in the implementation. It helps if the senior management team are committed as well. For this reason, most organisations start by having a board or senior management presentation and discussion on Team Briefing at one of their meetings.

The union representatives need to know about Team Briefing and be able to ask questions about it. The system does not directly involve union representatives (except in so far as they are all members of a team somewhere). However, it is courtesy and common sense to inform them; if this does not happen there can be considerable reaction to the perceived threat. Sometimes, a union presentation takes place, other times it becomes an item on the agenda of an existing meeting.

Commitment from each manager and supervisor who is going to brief is important. This is one of the key objectives of a course for all briefers to be held before briefing starts.

Co-ordinator

Once there is senior management commitment, the responsibility for setting up the system needs to be given to a co-ordinator. The person should have the time to spend on the project, but be senior enough to have some influence. Preferably, they need to know the organisation structure and accountability within it. The Managing Director rarely has the time or detailed day to day knowledge to make it worth doing personally (although the managing directors have co-ordinated in some smaller companies). Normally it is more likely to be the Personnel or Staff Manager, the Communication Manager, occasionally the Factory Manager.

Advice and help from outside are a tremendous advantage. The co-ordinator supplies the internal drive and knowledge—the outsider brings credibility and experience from a knowledge of other organisations' systems and can see the 'wood for the trees' by being able to be more objective. The two are a good team—but the role does not exclude or rule out the role of the other. If the co-ordinator does not report directly to the Managing Director or Chief Executive, it is necessary for them to have direct access for Team Briefing matters. See Appendix 1 for details of

one possible programme for introducing Team Briefing to briefers.
The role of the co-ordinator is to:

—set up the stage of implementation for the system and make sure they take place properly and within the set timescale. There is an example of a co-ordinator's time plan for implementation in Appendix 2.

—maintain the system once it is running (see final chapter on 'Making sure it does not fail').

Structure and Drill

Team Briefing will not "just happen" if the Managing Director says it should. There needs to be a structure and drill that can be monitored. The structure makes sure that everyone knows who briefs whom in which teams and the drill lays down when it should happen and how often. Team Briefing is based on five basic principles. When making decisions about setting up the system, the principles need to be used as guidance. The structure and drill for each organisation will differ—but the following points are fundamental to any system.

Team Briefing is:

Face to face	Regular
In teams	Relevant
By the leader	

• *Face to face*

Talking to people face to face is the only way of being sure that they have heard and understood. You cannot ask a piece of paper a question—in fact you cannot even guarantee that most people will read it in the first place. Credibility of the message comes from the more personal approach; it is much easier to motivate people face to face than by memo.

• *In Teams*

Why not talk to each person individually? Well, of course, good managers will regularly talk to their people on an individual basis about things that affect the individual. Briefing is an opportunity to talk to the team about things that affect all of them. There are advantages in doing it:

- It is quicker, particularly with a large team, to talk to all at once.
- It makes sure that you do not forget people occasionally when you are 'doing the rounds'.
- *You* know and *they* know that you have told them all the same story! With the best will and intentions in the world, it is virtually impossible to tell the same story to ten different people. It is easy to breed mistrust when information is compared (as it usually is); management is accused of manipulation inevitably.
- The potential for understanding is far greater in a group than with an individual. If one person asks a question, the entire group benefits from the answer; other members may not have thought of the question or may be too retiring to ask. On the other hand, a member of the group

may have understood the wrong thing and not realised it until someone else's questioning highlights the error.

- The 'work team' meeting together is a great group motivator. It reinforces the fact that the team is working together towards common objectives.

The team needs to be small but not too small; 4-15 in a group is ideal. Sample briefs are in Appendices 4 and 5.

• ***By the leader***

The briefer must be accountable for the performance of the group being briefed; he or she is the work group leader. Sometimes this may make it logical to make the Team Briefing structure differ from the organisation's hierarchy. For instance, where there is a maintenance department, it could be more sensible to brief the engineers with the lines that they normally work on, than with each other. Briefing then becomes more production orientated—although it means that their direct 'boss' is not briefing. Where people report to more than one manager—with perhaps a task/function split—it is important to specify the briefer carefully. Obviously a task orientated group is preferable if it is possible.

The choice of briefers can be affected by a team size, which is very important. If there are fewer than three in a team, the benefits of group interaction are lost. In this case, it may be a better solution to use the 'grandfather' to brief; they are still accountable one rung further up the ladder. So in the example below—the manager would brief all the people in the diagram.

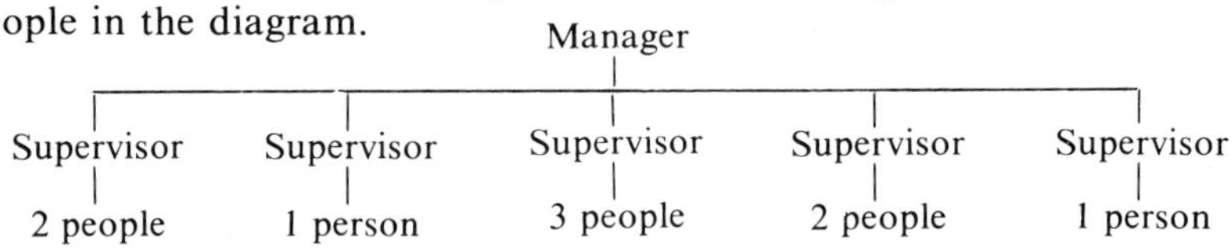

Small teams are a common problem in white collar departments and commercial companies. Obviously, teams that are too large are equally difficult. If the group is more than fifteen strong communication becomes increasingly difficult and the team harder to control. In this case briefing can be passed down rather than upwards. This can be done by using existing chargehands (or their equivalent)—or getting existing supervisors to brief more than once and split their teams. In the example this would mean either the manager briefs the supervisors and chargehands together and the chargehands brief on or the manager briefs the supervisors who will brief twice. For example:

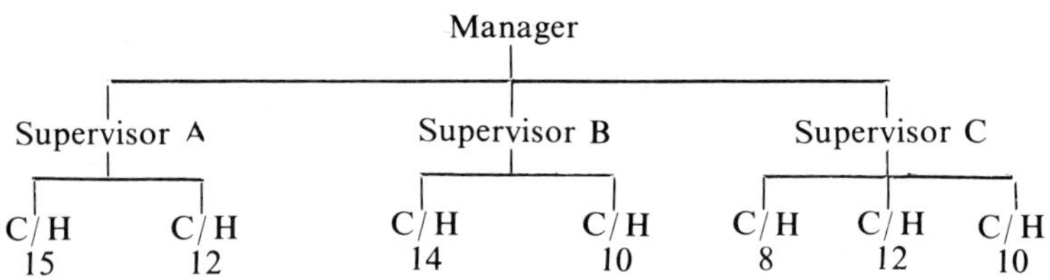

In some cases it would be advisable for Supervisor C in the example to brief three times if all the groups are doing different work.

Large teams are usually a shop floor problem. It can be considerably confused by shifts! Unless there is a supervisor on each shift this normally means using the chargehands. Structuring the system can be complicated when trying to choose leaders and teams which fit together and are the right size! However, wherever possible, the structure is based on the accountable workgroup leader at whatever level.

• ***Regular***

Most organisations brief monthly because it is related to the board or senior management meetings, which in turn relate to the accounting period for the organisation. The frequency may vary from company to company, but the regularity does not. In other words, briefing is not an *ad hoc* activity. It also tends to become ineffective if it is not held at least every month. Regularity breeds credibility.

• ***Relevant***

Good local information is the key to relevance. However it is not enough just to ask people to add local information to the senior management brief. In practice very few bother to do it, and the briefing will very quickly become just the senior management brief. What is required is a drill to ensure that there is a high level of local input. As mentioned above at least seventy per cent of the brief should be local information, with only thirty per cent coming from above.

An engineering company in Glasgow came up with a simple drill to solve this problem. They require their supervisors to prepare their own briefing notes prior to their meeting with their managers. A couple of days before the main procedures start, the supervisors write down those points which they want to brief their own teams on. They then talk those points through with their managers, or show them their written brief. The manager then adds, when he is briefing the supervisors, any points that have come from senior management or from himself. The whole emphasis of the brief is turned around. In each case the brief given by the supervisor is the local brief prepared by him, with some senior management points added. Far from acting as a parrot for senior management, he is putting across his own information. This not only makes all the difference to the effectiveness of briefing, it also means that the senior management points are put across with greater enthusiasm and commitment by the supervisor.

The key then to relevant briefing is that at each level managers and supervisors should prepare their own local points, before being briefed by the level above, and have those local points checked. One of the simplest ways of doing this is to require briefers to come to the meeting where they are briefed, with their local people present, and ask them for their local points. This provides a very effective means of checking that the local points are prepared; it also gives the manager some valuable feedback on what the local issues are of the next level down; finally each briefer hears the points that are going to be put across by his colleagues providing valuable cross fertilisation of ideas.

This checking of local points is a crucial element of turning the briefing from an often irrelevant cascade system, into Team Briefing with all the benefits that that brings in terms of people's effectiveness at the point of work. Making managers and supervisors prepare local points, is often an up hill battle; however with perserverance you will succeed. Just one of the benefits is that you are getting supervisors to sit down once a month to consider how the job is going and how the job can be done better, in effect getting them to think as managers.

In addition to applying these five main principles, there are some other important points to take into account.

Levels

If information from the senior meeting has to cascade through many levels, the end result will be something akin to chinese whispers! If the facts are going to stand a chance of being transmitted and explained similarly throughout the organisation, it is wise to structure with no more than four levels from top to bottom. If there are too many levels, it is often a case of small teams at middle levels—so if you follow the advice on the leader and team size, there should not be a problem. If it seems impossible, and your organisation is very large, can it be split into smaller operating units by task or site for the briefing exercise? Levels should be split up from the bottom, the front line—i.e. the work group leader is of course the most important. Below is an example of four standard levels in a standard company structure.

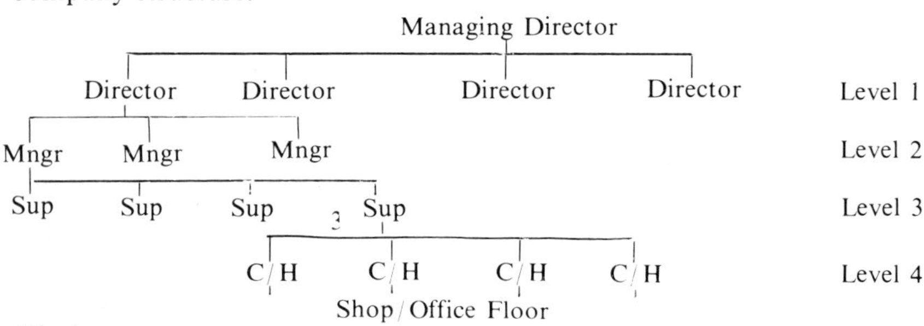

Timing

Obviously, it is important for briefing to take place at a set time. To make sure that it happens, most organisations set dates for a year ahead. All the teams need to be briefed within 48 hours if at all possible. This prevents the grapevine from passing the information on before the later briefing gets a chance to do so.

It is also advisable to brief each level at the same time. The majority of employees will be at level four. When sorting out the timing, it is a good idea to start by setting a time at which everyone can be briefed at once at this level. Obviously, this can mean stopping production for half an hour altogether: this can be more convenient than various people stopping at odd times. The time of day at which this happens needs to be chosen carefully to make it most effective and least disruptive. Chargehands can normally come up with the solution here.

When shifts are involved, they need to be briefed separately, but as close as possible to each other. Often it is possible to brief two shifts together—one before it goes off and the other as it is coming on. Continuous process is often very difficult. Sometimes it is possible to leave a skeleton maintenance team on the machines while the rest are briefed. These operators are then briefed afterwards. There are different solutions for different situations, but clearly they do not involve stopping the process.

Most organisations do not have 'ideal' structures for Team Briefing. Bearing in mind the points above for guidance, the aim is to arrive at the best solution possible and not expect perfection!

Paperwork

Paperwork should be kept to a minimum. However, a number of documents provide invaluable back up.

- ***A policy document.*** This sets out for all employees the approach to Team Briefing and how it will work. It includes the structure and drill, clearly laid out for all to see. This is the 'bible' for the system and obviously needs to be regularly revised when people leave or there is any internal restructuring. For an example, see the policy document in Appendix 3.
- ***Briefing forms.*** It is useful to keep a record of each brief for reference. For the company brief it enables each briefer to have back-up notes with exactly the same key facts on them. In smaller companies (under 60) it may not be necessary to use a formal written back-up brief. Normally, the only typed brief that briefers receive is the one that emanates from the Senior Management meeting. This has a couple of key points on it. Briefers all receive a copy of this through the line brief session. In addition, they keep blank copies of forms to write their local briefs on. See Appendix 4 for examples of briefing forms.
- ***Briefing folders.*** It helps to give each briefer a folder to keep these papers together and any notes that he or she wants to keep during the month that need to be dealt with at the meeting—a sort of *aide memoire*.
- ***Feedback forms.*** In a larger company, getting answers to questions through the system can be a problem. If supervisors do not know the answer to a question about an item on the company brief, it is important that they should say "I'm sorry, I don't know the answer but I'll note the question and find out for you". If the system is to be credible at all, it is most important that these answers are forthcoming and quick. Often the questions and answers get 'lost' in the system as the reply never comes back or it is distorted or it takes months! Two days is the maximum length of time to aim at for getting answers back to questions. A feed back form is helpful to make sure that this happens. See Appendix 7 for a Feedback Form.

Normally, if supervisors cannot answer a question, they note it on the feedback from and send a copy to their immediate 'boss' and one to the co-ordinator. It is the co-ordinator's job to make sure that the supervisor gets an answer. If the immediate manager cannot answer it either, the co-ordinator has direct access to the Managing Director or most Senior Manager, who supplies the answer. The system allows the co-ordinator to keep a record of the sort of questions that are being asked throughout the organisation. This is helpful feedback for future briefs. Remember though, questions should only be those relating to the subject matter of the brief—not any questions that anyone wants to ask; if there is no control, the feedback can become unmanageable.

These are the key paperwork documents to back up the system. The only other paper is that which is connected to the training courses.

Training

A good system with a solid structure and drill is like a good machine; it will not work properly unless there is a trained operator to make it work. Training the briefers is critical in making Team Briefing effective. The courses need to cover the following:

Explaining why the company is putting the system in.
What is Team Briefing?
How will the structure and drill work in this organisation?
What to talk about at the meeting—how to prepare local information.
Attending a briefing meeting—asking the right questions—taking notes, adding the company brief to the local notes.

Presenting a brief:

- putting it across clearly.
- answering questions.
- maintaining control.
- keeping interest.
- dealing with difficult people or situations.

Practice in presenting a brief for each person with advice.

The course is designed to achieve three objectives:

- To gain commitment to the system of Team Briefing
- To get understanding of how the system operates and why
- To assist briefers in the skills of preparing and giving a brief.

All briefers need to be trained—if possible on courses of mixed 'levels'. There is an example of a typical two day course programme in Appendix 1.

Starting to brief

Once the training is completed, briefing can start on the date selected. This needs to be as soon as possible after the courses, so that the impetus is not lost. The top management information for the first brief should be 'meaty' but not too contentious! Some companies prefer to start with a 'dry run' down to supervisor level only to test the structure before going all the way. This enables some of the problems to be ironed out initially.

5 What to talk about

Relevant
The important point to remember is that in each Team Briefing the information must be *relevant*. This normally means that at shop-floor level or office-floor level, about 70% should be about the work and everyday events of that team—about 30% should come from above, information about the division, the region, the company or even, sometimes, the Group. This other information is useful to put the local information into context and also to remind people that there is a larger 'team' that they are all working for. It also enables senior management to pass on important information when it is needed and be able to be sure that everyone has been told—but there is unlikely to be a great deal of this on a monthly basis, unless the company is going through a crisis.

Need/Want
Team Briefing enables managers to communicate information that people *need* to know—that *management* need them to know. It is not designed to entertain. Some briefers become quite neurotic about trying to find something that people are interested in and *want* to know about. This unfortunately gives the team the idea that it is a little break for them, rather than of any real purpose. Do not expect the workforce to be ecstatic with interest or riveted to their seats—if they are not, it does not mean that Team Briefing is failing.

> ***Example:***
> Several years ago, I was working at a construction company, training a group of site foremen. Team Briefing had been operating for a few years—but everybody always grumbled that it was boring and that all it was good for was a break from work. Everyone moaned once a month without fail. But, fate dealt a blow to the system, when the company was taken over by a group whose Chief Executive did not believe in communication; he immediately disbanded the system. Ironically, while I was running the training course, all anybody talked about was how dreadful it was that briefing had stopped and could I do anything about it because they had forgotten what it was like to be continually in the dark! Typically briefing is something that people take for granted!

Subject matter
Information about the company from the Board of Directors or senior management team, is passed to everyone, so that all hear the same story. To make this more effective, there is normally a typed brief with the main points for people to brief from. All briefers receive this. Information added in at each successive level is written by the individual briefer. This works

as long as there are not too many levels for the information to pass through (this has been discussed in an earlier chapter).

Subject matter can be classified easily under four points:

PROGRESS
POLICY
PEOPLE
POINTS FOR ACTION

• ***Progress***

There should always be progress. This section is about 'how we are doing' either as a company or a team. Are we meeting targets? What are we going to try and achieve next month? That is, 'This is where we are and that is where we are going'. 'Progress' is much more effective as an item if there are regular 'yardsticks' of performance that people can measure themselves against; e.g. quality level, wastage levels, cost savings, units produced, rework, downtime, meeting delivery dates, etc. If quality is the most important area for people to concentrate on, there should always be an item on quality and how we are doing.

• ***Policy***

Changes in policies or procedures at company or local level. The example earlier of the change in invoice procedure is an obvious one here. Reinforcing existing policies or procedures that people may have forgotten is useful as well: for instance, the grievance procedure.

• ***People***

This section is fairly obvious. Anything to do with changes to do with people: new employees, people retiring, long service, visitors to the factory, promotions, job changes, etc.

• ***Points for action***

Anything that you want people to do e.g. keeping the office tidy, being more safety conscious on the shop-floor, filling forms in more accurately, etc.

The four P's are used as memory joggers by briefers—often a topic could fit under more than one heading. It is not important to get an item under the 'right' heading—it is important to remember to talk about it. We asked a number of companies who briefed to list the sort of topics they have used under each of the four P's and compiled a list*. It is clear that the four P's can be used either at top level or at the level of first line supervision; the principles are the same—the nature of the material may vary. So that under progress, the company yardstick might be the number of orders, whereas on the line it might be the number of units produced; same principles, different emphasis.

---

*It is useful to see the sort of headings they come up with. The list is contained in 'A briefer's guide to team briefing' by Rupert Middleton also published by The Industrial Society. Your organisation will, of course, have topics of its own to add!

Use examples:
The meeting will be more interesting and more relevant if practical examples are used rather than abstract theory being discussed.

e.g. ***Abstract theory*** . . . "I think our safety standards have slipped and we must all make an effort to pull our socks up because safety is very important."

Practical example . . . "Last week George nearly broke his leg when he fell over a box that had been left in the gangway. If we don't keep those passageways clear someone will break their neck."

Good and bad news
Bad news is not popular, but it has to be told. On the other hand, it is very easy to turn a briefing meeting into a group discipline session if you are not careful. Good news always seems harder to remember and much of it has been forgotten by the time briefing arrives! It is important to make a note of good things when they happen: extra hard work, other departments' help, a letter of praise etc. If there is no good news then talk about things in a positive rather than negative way.

e.g. ***Negative*** . . . We didn't meet our targets last month, in fact we failed by over 50%, we did really badly."

Positive . . . "Although we failed to meet our targets by over 50% last month, there is no reason why we can't pick up some of the loss next month and break even by the end of the year, if we . . ."

In other words if there is bad, why?—and what is being done about it? At local level, what can *we* do about it?

For an example of a real company brief and a brief written by a first line surpervisor, turn to Appendix 4 and 5.

No new news isn't bad news
It is a common misunderstanding that everything briefed must be 'new' in order to be 'interesting'. The objective is to inform on a regular basis but that normally means at a monthly meeting, the only real 'new' information will be whatever happened yesterday! Some people have been known to 'save up' information and keep it secret until briefing so that they could announce it! Good managers communicate with their staff on a day to day basis—this has to happen for the job to be done. Day to day communication, however, is much more haphazard and tends to be frenetic—there is little opportunity to stand back and put action into perspective. At briefing we can look back at the total picture that has been built up and look forward to the overall picture that lies ahead. If you compare communicating to a film—day to day communication is a bit like looking in detail at each frame of the film at a time. Briefing is when all those frames are run through the projector and a total picture emerges; it is

also where we get a quick preview of the next month's film—so that when we need to look in detail at each individual frame, we have already seen the film and can put it more easily into context and priority.

Briefing also gives managers and supervisors an opportunity to brief the 'official news'. People may have already heard it from several sources on the grapevine, but briefing is management's way of saying that this is the 'real' news. It may confirm what people already know but give a more full explanation of the situation. Above all, it allows employees to ask questions about the information as a team and it makes sure that management *know* that everyone has been told.

New information is briefed at the meeting but if there is no totally 'new' news—it does not mean that Team Briefing has failed!

6 Making sure it does not fail

Just as a machine needs maintenance, so a Team Briefing system needs monitoring. The co-ordinator needs to prompt and encourage monitoring, but the most important part of it is done by the line management at *each level,* including senior management (especially the Chief Executive). There are a number of ways of monitoring effectively.

A clear company policy on Team Briefing with clearly defined accountability for who does what is in Appendix 3.

Checking local briefs

This is especially important in the first few months when briefers may not be sure about their own input. Some companies do this during the briefing meeting. The manager asks each supervisor to quickly run through their local points. This takes time and so briefs are often checked prior to the meeting. A few days before briefing staff, the supervisors prepare their notes (key points, not essays) and send them to their manager. If the manager does not respond that will be the final brief.

Walking the job

This is the most important type of monitoring and it should be carried out by the management line from the most senior level down. Managers walk around and talk to people informally to check how much they know. Obviously, this should not be seen as an attempt to by-pass local management—so should be done with their knowledge. It is best to ask specific questions, for instance: David Plastow, Managing Director of Vickers plc, tends to ask three questions when he visits a company and walks the job on the shop floor. "What is your order book like?" "Who told you?" "When were you told?".

These questions are simple but effective in testing the system. For some further guidance on walking the job, see Appendix 6.

Training

After the initial training for briefers, it is essential for the co-ordinator to watch for new appointments or re-organisations which will produce new briefers. These should be given some guidance to help them by their managers and the co-ordinator.

Reviews

It is very helpful to hold regular reviews of the system to identify and solve all problems or to improve the existing arrangements. Groups of supervisors and groups of managers can be called on to review meetings.

Obviously, this is done with co-operation from the line management. It is also useful to have a recurring item on the board or senior management meeting agenda twice a year.

In many other organisations, there is a monthly supervisors' review. After each brief—all the supervisors get back together, with their managers to feed back and to review the briefing.

All of the above methods are useful once the system is running effectively. During the first year—it is advisable to check it more throughly. The first critical stage is after three months, when the 'teething' problems of a new system start to show. A full review at this stage can prevent problems from getting worse and reinforce the successful areas of Team Briefing. It also makes sure that it is actually happening and not just a case of paying 'lipservice'.

After six months, the 'honeymoon phase' is over. It is no longer new and there is not the back-log of 'easy' information to talk about. This is the most likely time for interest to wane. A review now can stop the system from falling apart. It reinforces to management that this is not just going to be a 'fad' that senior management will forget about, but something that will be part of the management style.

After 12 months, Team Briefing will have become normal management practice. It will happen automatically and continue as long as the monitoring mentioned at the beginning of the chapter is carried out.

Making sure it does not fail is also about development of feedback. A better informed workforce is always more keen to express views and ideas and become involved. Information stimulates interest and it is an enormous advantage to the organisation that can harness it. Often, the introduction of Quality Circles, that identify and solve problems in their own work area, can be a very successful follow-up to Team Briefing. So can revitalising the consultation committee to make it more effective and allowing training managers and supervisors to hold Team Meetings to ask for vital opinions about decisions that affect the team.

Team Briefing lays the foundations for the development of employees, involvement at work. If management is unaware of the need for this, there can be despondency after a period of time because management seems to only be interested in 'telling' and not 'listening'. Team Briefing cannot be both the downward and upward channel for communication, but it is the start point from which the upward channel can be developed through separate meetings.

The future of this country depends on involving people in their work. We will only get that commitment from them if they are fully informed about what is happening in the organisation and their position in it. The Industrial Society knows that many organisations have many different ways of communicating with their people. However, there is no doubt that Team Briefing is the most effective method. Team Briefing lays the foundations for the development of employee involvement at work.

APPENDIX 1

British Telecom Team Briefing two-day training course

DAY ONE

0900 Introduction

Session 1: **Why Communication Matters**

How it affects the efficiency of an organisation
Film: "The Grapevine"
Group discussion: How communication slip-ups have affected the company.

Session 2: **Team Briefing—Overview**

Benefits of communicating through meetings
Principles of Team Briefing, and barriers
The manager's responsibility for communication
The need for a drill

Session 3: **How the drill will work**

Who/When/Where; Paperwork; Answering Questions

Session 4: **Subjects**

Syndicate groups and report back

Session 5: **Preparing a Local Brief**

1 What and How
2 Delegates will prepare their own briefs

1700 END OF DAY

British Telecom Team Briefing two-day training course *continued*

DAY TWO

0900 Review of Day One

Session 6: **Being Briefed**

1 Note taking, questioning
2 Making information relevant to the team
3 Practice session in briefing—a manager will brief the other delegates on the "company brief"

Session 7: **Briefing**

1 Format of the meeting
2 Skills of putting it across

Session 8: **Practice Session in Briefing**

Role plays of briefing meetings. All delegates will brief the rest of the group on prepared topics

Session 9: **Following-up, Monitoring**

Steps to keep the system operating and live

Action session

1700 END OF COURSE

APPENDIX 2

Draft plan for introducing Team Briefing at T.I. Gas Spares—Spring 1982

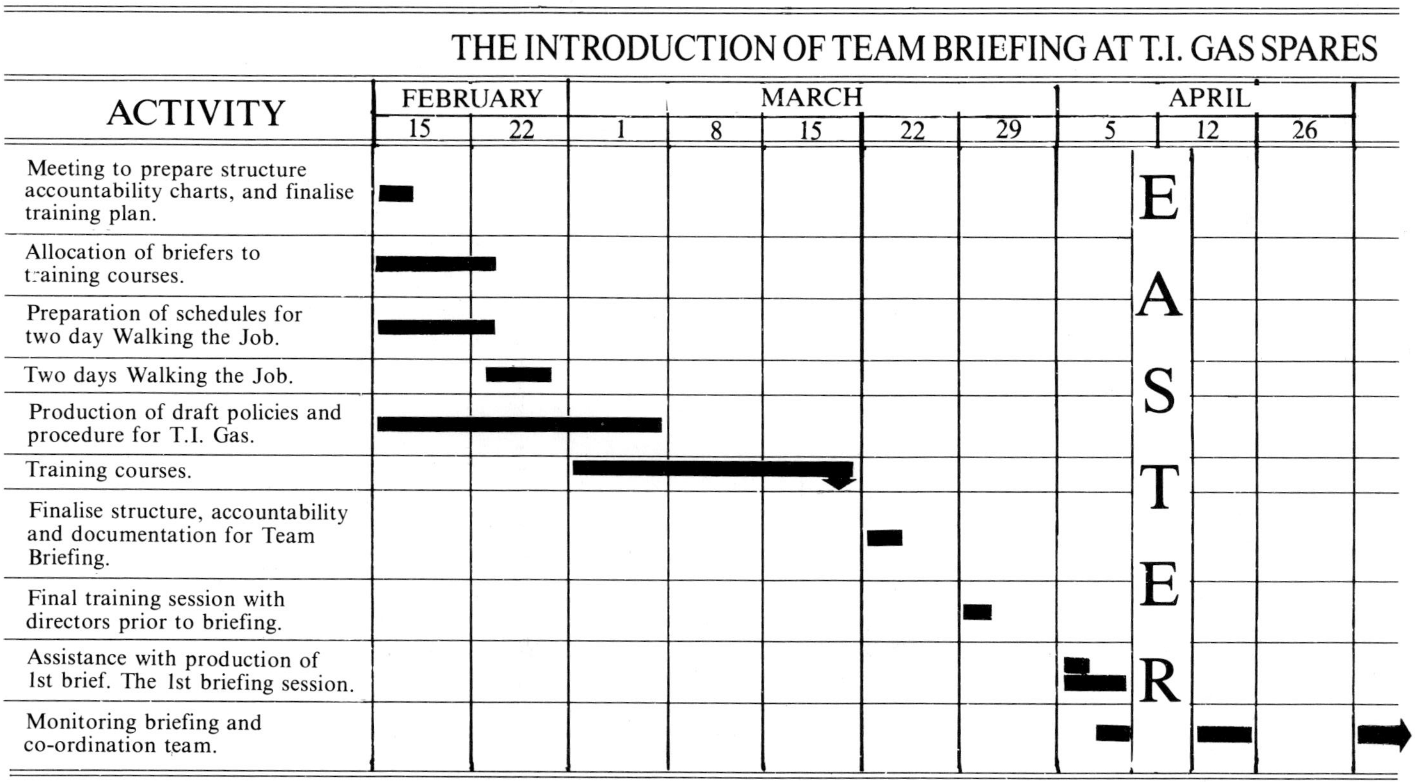

NOTE: Dates shown indicate actual dates for the activity.
I McDOUGALL SENIOR ADVISER COMMUNICATION DEPT.

APPENDIX 3

Brown Brothers & Company Limited
Rosebank Works—Edinburgh

Communication—Team Briefing

1 In recognition of the importance of communicating Company and Departmental information regularly and accurately, 'Team Briefing' was introduced, effective from March 1982.

2 'Team Briefing' is a systematic approach to communication, through meetings held at regular intervals, with opportunities for questions and answers.

3 Aims of 'Team Briefing' are to:

(a) Minimise misunderstandings
(b) Seek co-operation
(c) Improve commitment
(d) Reinforce role of manager/supervisor
(e) Reduce damaging effect of rumour

4 Teams, or Briefing Groups, should, ideally, consist of between 4 and 15 people, from work teams with a common identity.

5 Team Leader, or Briefer, will usually be the line manager or supervisor accountable for the work of the team.

6 Items to talk about may be categorised under the following guidance headings:

(a) Progress
(b) Policy
(c) People
(c) Points for action

7 Briefers will ensure that information is relevant and that it contains 'local' information prepared by the Briefer. All subjects will be recorded on the 'Management Brief' Form.

8 Briefers will also record names of absentees and be responsible for briefing them when available.

9 The Company Management Reporting Structure forms the basis of the Briefing Group Structure.

10 Briefing Groups will be held on Monday, Tuesday and Wednesday of, generally the fourth week of each of the following nine months.

February	May	September
March	June	October
April	August	November

11 On the last Briefing Group of the year, lists of Team Briefing dates for the next year will be issued to each employee.

12 Briefing Groups, defining names of Leaders, Deputies, Venues, Days and times of the team meetings are listed.

Technical Administration Manager.

Brown Brothers & Company Limited
Rosebank Works—Edinburgh

Team Briefing—Dates for 1983

	Monday	Tuesday	Wednesday
January		No meetings	
February	21st	22nd	23rd
March	28th	29th	30th
April	25th	26th	27th
May	23rd	24th	25th
June	27th	28th	29th
July		No meetings	
August	22nd	23rd	24th
September	26th	27th	28th
October	24th	25th	26th
November	28th	29th	30th
December		No meetings	

Briefing groups

Briefing Group Number	Leader	Deputy	Venue	Day	Time
1	C K Benington	Ad Hoc (Director)	Board Room	Mon	11.30am
2	R H Gardiner	A Macmillan	Financial Director's Room	Mon	4.15pm
3	A Macmillan	R H Gardiner	Conference Room No. 2	Tues	4.15pm
4	H Spence	R H Gardiner	Commercial Office	Tues	4.15pm
5	G McDermid	R H Gardiner	Computer Room	Tues	4.15pm
6	J T Hatleskog	R J Donaldson	Technical Director's Room	Mon	4.15pm
7	S K Bjørkly	R Wragg	General Manager's (CSD) Room	Tues	3.00pm
8	R Wragg	S Berrington	Production Department (CSD)	Wed	10.30am
9	I Smith	S K Bjørkly	Laboratory, (CSD)	Wed	10.30am
10	I Wilson	S K Bjørkly	Drawing Office (CSD)	Wed	10.30am
11	R J Donaldson	J Till	Publications Office (2nd Floor North)	Tues	3.00pm
12	A C Fairlie-Clarke	S Coward	R & D Office (2nd Floor South)	Tues	3.00pm
13A	I Gibb	J Till	Production D.O. (North)	Tues	3.00pm
13B	W Gibb	J Till	Production D.O. (South)	Tues	3.00pm
14	W Inglis	D J McNeill	Sales Director's Room (also by correspondence)	Mon	4.15pm
15	A Pottinger	W Reid G Leith	Production Director's Room	Mon	4.15pm
16	G Leith	W Blacklaws	Production Services Manager's Room	Tues	4.15pm
17	W Blacklaws	G Leith	Conference Room No. 2	Wed	9.30am
18	C Ratcliffe	G Leith	General Stores	Wed	2.45pm
19	A Niven	G Leith	Production Engineering Section	Wed	2.45pm
20	J Andrews	G Leith	Programming Section	Wed	2.45pm
21	W Reid	P Lawson*	Work Manager's Room (Meeting will be held at 1.45pm on Management Committee Meeting days)	Tues	11.30am or 1.45pm
22	J Allan	P Lawson*	Head Foreman's Room (Fitting Shop)	Tues	4.15pm
23	S Lawrie	P Lawson*	Plant Department (Electrical)	Wed	9.45am
24	J Ewing	P Lawson*	Test House	Wed	2.45 pm
25	J Munro	P Lawson*	Lower Locker Room (Fitting Shop)	Wed	9.45am
26	M Wilson	P Lawson*	Light Fitting Shop	Wed	2.45pm
27			Upper Locker Room (Fitting Shop)		
28	A Hogg	P Lawson*	Locker Room (Welding Shop)	Wed	9.45am
29	D Forbes	P Lawson*	Locker Room (Welding Shop)	Wed	2.45pm
30	G Leslie	P Lawson*	Pattern Shop	Wed	9.45am
31	A McKenzie	P Lawson*	Head Foreman's (Machine Shop) Room	Tues	4.15pm
32	A Mckenzie	P Lawson*	Tool Room	Wed	2.45pm
33A	J Bowman	P Lawson*	Conference Room No. 1	Wed	9.45am
33B	J Bowman	P Lawson*	Conference Room No. 1	Wed	2.45pm
34A	A Robertson	P Lawson*	R & D Area (Gallery)	Wed	9.45am
34B	A Robertson	P Lawson*	R & D Area (Gallery)	Wed	2.45pm
35A	K Stokes	P Lawson*	No. 1 Locker Room (Machine Shop)	Wed	9.45am
35B	K Stokes	P Lawson*	No. 1 Locker Room (Machine Shop)	Wed	2.45pm
36	J Hughes	P Lawson*	Lower Locker Room (Fitting Shop)	Wed	11.30am
37	K Harding	T Blyth	Plant Engineer's Room	Tues	4.15pm
38	T Blyth	K Harding	Plant Department (Mechanical)	Wed	9.45am
39	G Dick	J B Smith	Quality Manager's Office	Tues	3.00pm
40	A Ballach	J B Smith	Head Foreman's (Inspection) Office	Wed	2.45pm
41	T Henderson	J B Smith	Ex Electrical Area	Wed	2.45pm
42	R Kerr	D Cooper	Service Department (also by correspondence)	Tues	3.00pm
43	G D Crichton	D Irvine	Personnel Manager's Room	Tues	4.15pm
44	D Irvine	G Prentice	Training Officer's Room	Wed	4.15pm
45	J Smith	G D Crichton	Security Officer's Room	Wed	5.30pm
46	G Prentice	D Irvine	Training Department School Room	Wed	2.45pm
47	G D Crichton	D Irvine	By correspondence	Wed	—
48	R B Rae	R Hay I McOwan I G Ross	Commercial Director's Room	Mon	4.15pm
49	R Hay	F Lorimer	Estimating Department	Tues	1.30pm
50	I McOwan	A McMinn	Purchasing Department	Wed	10.30am
51	I G Ross	J Henderson	Contracts Department	Tues	1.30pm

*K Harding in P Lawson's Absence

Briefing group structure

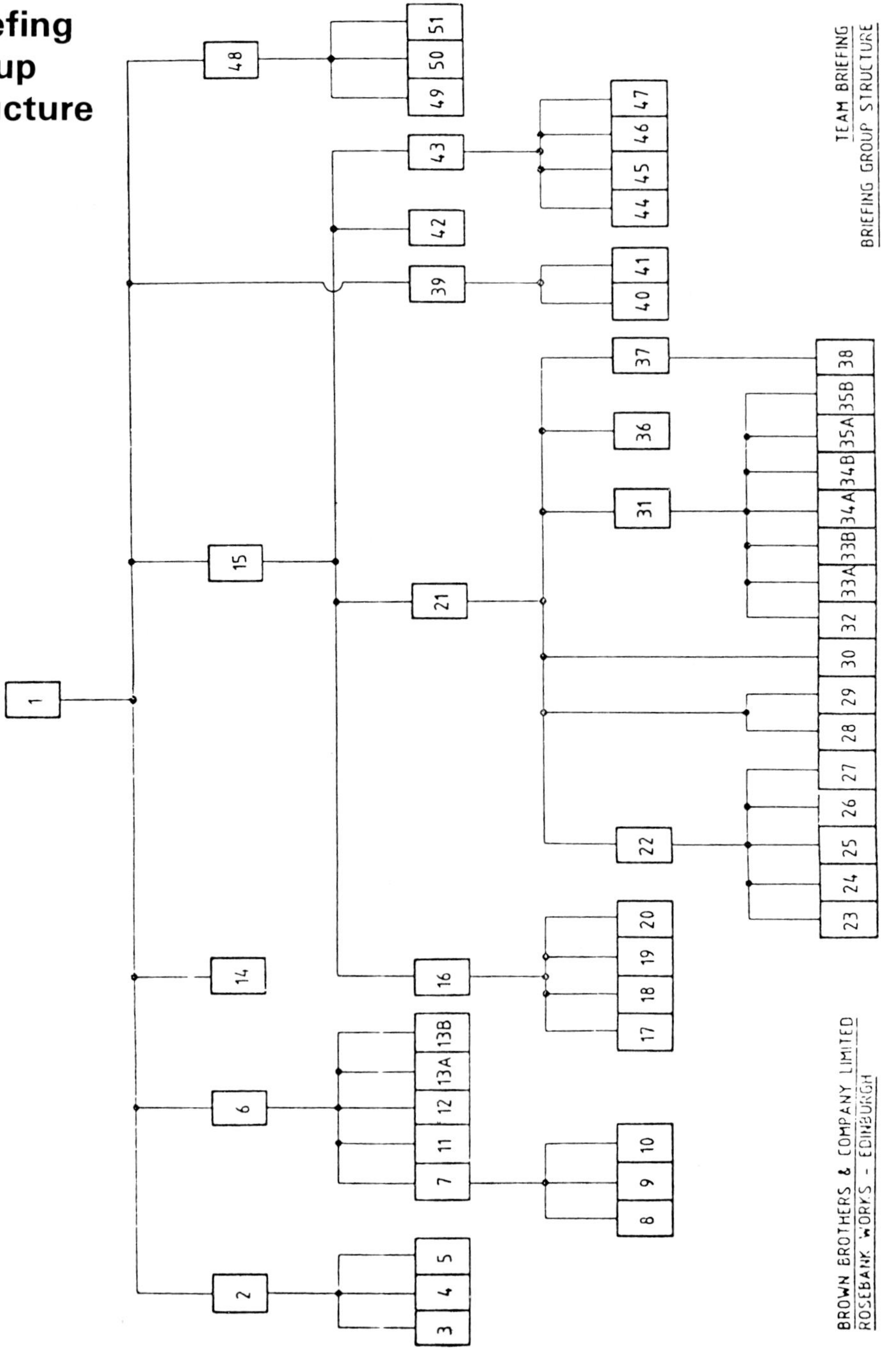

Accountability chart

- C. K. BENINGTON
MANAGING DIRECTOR
  - R. H. GARDINER
FINANCIAL DIRECTOR
    - A. MACMILLAN
ACCOUNTANT
      - H. SPENCE
COMMERCIAL OFFICE MANAGER
      - W. MALCOLM
FINANCIAL CONTROL MANAGER
    - G. McDERMID
DATA PROCESSING MANAGER
  - J. T. HATLESKOG
TECHNICAL DIRECTOR
    - S. K. BJORKLY
GENERAL MANAGER C.S.D.
      - R. WRAGG
PRODUCTION MANAGER C.S.D.
      - I. SMITH
PROJECT MANAGER
    - R. J. DONALDSON
TECH. ADMINISTRATION MANAGER
      - I. BURNETT
PROJECT MANAGER
    - H. BROWN
PROGRAMME MANAGER
    - D. FISHER
CONSULTANT
    - A. C. FAIRLIE-CLARKE
DESIGN & DEVELOPMENT MANAGER
      - S. COWARD
DEV. MANAGER
      - J. McCANN
DES. MANAGER
      - J. FLATMAN
TEST MANAGER
    - I. GIBB
PRODUCT MANAGER
    - J. TILL
CHIEF ENGINEER
      - W. GIBB
PROJECT MANAGER
  - W. INGLIS
SALES DIRECTOR
    - D. J. McNEIL
SALES MANAGER
  - A. POTTINGER
PRODUCTION DIRECTOR
    - G. LEITH
PRODUCTION SERVICES MANAGER
      - W. BLACKLAWS
PRODUCTION CONTROL MANAGER
    - W. REID
WORKS MANAGER
      - P. LAWSON
WORKS SUPERINTENDENT
      - K. HARDING
PLANT ENGINEER
    - W. MOORE
PROJECT MANAGER
    - G. CRICHTON
PERSONNEL MANAGER
    - R. KERP
SERVICE MANAGER
  - R. B. RAE
COMMERCIAL DIRECTOR
    - R. HAY
ESTIMATING MANAGER
    - I. McOWAN
PURCHASING MANAGER
    - I. G. ROSS
CONTRACTS MANAGER
  - G. DICK
QUALITY MANAGER
    - J. SMITH
INSPECTION MANAGER

APPENDIX 4

Management brief

Briefing Group: 16 *Absentees:* S. PRICE & A. SIMMONS

Date and time briefing held: 16th JANUARY 1983-10 a.m. S. NEWBURY

Briefing Group Leader: J. B. SMITH

Note to Briefing Leader

1 This brief provides the essential message—add this information to your own briefing material.

2 Convey the meaning in your own words, which you know will be understood, and where possible illustrate with a practical example that is relevant to them.

3 Words or phrases which need to convey a precise meaning will be underlined. These should **not** be changed in briefing.

4 Encourage questions. Ensure that the message is understood.

5 Where possible give the answers to anticipated questions. Relate these to local situations. If you do not know the answer, say no, get the answer and give it to the questioner within 48 hours.

SUBJECTS AND KEY POINTS	NOTES
Sales: REACH TARGET FOR 1982 OF £7.5m. FORECAST 1983, PERIOD 1, £700,000. PLANNED INTAKE 1983 £8.3m.	
Orders: TYPE 22-09-22112. WHICH WILL TAKE US THROUGH TO 1985 40 + BLADES.	
Suggestion scheme: RE-INTRODUCING SCHEME. DETAILS LATER.	
Overheads: PROPOSED RATE INCREASE OF 40% WHICH MEANS AN EXTRA £60,000 PER YEAR.	

QUESTIONS ASKED	ANSWERS GIVEN – date

APPENDIX 5

Stone Vickers

Local brief

Dep't/Section Blade Finishing Briefing Group Leader G. W. PRYKE

Location LOCKER ROOM Date & Time 18TH JANUARY 1983 - 10AM

Brief Originated By G. W. PRYKE Those Absent

Briefing Group Number 16

Work in Progress

Still very heavy 7CA666 etc.
XS665
XL670

New Patterns

XL670 LH. 1st off Block from new Pattern.
O.K. for Thickness + 4.0m x 6.0mm which is just right.
XL670 RH Pattern still incorrect. Sent back to Pattern makers for correction.

Swing Frame Grinding Machine

Latest information

Wall Lights

Latest Information

Repair Work

Plenty of Repair Blades outstanding.

NOTE TO BRIEFING GROUP LEADER

1. This brief provides the essential message.
2. Convey the meaning in your own words, which you know will be understood and where possible illustrate with a practical example.
3. Words or phrases which convey a precise meaning, difficult to express otherwise will be underlined. These should *not* be changed in briefing.
4. Encourage questions. Ensure that the message is understood.
5. Where possible the answers to anticipated questions will be given. Adapt these to local needs. If you don't know the answer, say so, get the answer and give it later to the questioner, or the group, whichever is necessary.

A Vickers company

Stone Vickers

Local brief *continued*

Dep't/Section Blade Finishing Briefing Group Leader G.W. PRYKIE

Location LOCKIER ROOM Date & Time 18TH JANUARY 1983. 10AM

Brief Originated By G.W. PRYKIE Those Absent

Briefing Group Number 16

Job Cards

Completed cards must be handed in each day.

Internal Quality Audit

Route Cards

Make sure all completed Ops are signed up. Also make sure you are working to latest drawings as stated on Route Card.

Finishing Times

Still needs to be greatly improved.

Canteen

Work still in progress and on time.

Social Club

Letter sent 7th Dec. 82 concerning Membership which will be discussed at next Club Committee Meeting.

NOTE TO BRIEFING GROUP LEADER

1. This brief provides the essential message.
2. Convey the meaning in your own words, which you know will be understood and where possible illustrate with a practical example.
3. Words or phrases which convey a precise meaning, difficult to express otherwise will be underlined. These should *not* be changed in briefing.
4. Encourage questions. Ensure that the message is understood.
5. Where possible the answers to anticipated questions will be given. Adapt these to local needs. If you don't know the answer, say so, get the answer and give it later to the questioner, or the group, whichever is necessary.

A Vickers company

APPENDIX 6

Checklist for action
Walking the job

The manager's ability to achieve results depends on gaining commitment to the job from other people. At all levels managers must monitor what is happening and be seen. The best way of doing this is walking the job.

1 Mark off adequate time for walking the job in the diary. Senior people should ensure their secretaries see all departments are included in the programmes so as to be covered periodically. Consider giving advance notice if visiting different locations.

2 Call to see the Head of Department as a courtesy so that he knows what is happening and on occasions can give information. Ask to see his accountability chart. Ask him such questions as 'Does he bring his team around him to talk about what has been achieved and what the targets are? How often is this done? How much absenteeism is there in the department? What is he doing about it?

3 Speak to people and ask them about their jobs:
What are they doing?
What are their achievements (against standards, targets?)
Do they know how their department is doing? (Is this week going to be above target?)
What was last month like here—up or down?
How can the job be done better?
Do they know who is their boss?

4 Get to know people. They will respond if their name is known but it is essential to get it right. Unless personal information is correct and up to date stick to talking about the job. They respect recognition of the imporatnce to the organisation of the job they are doing however humble.

5 Listen to people when they are prepared to talk about their successes or mistakes.

6 Be prepared to give praise and encouragement.

7 Make sure if faults are found or action is needed that the reprimand or instruction is to the person's immediate boss and not the individual.

8 Monitor that decisions taken higher up the organisation have been properly explained and understood.

9 Check the state of housekeeping and tidiness:

- Toilets
- Notice boards
- Target graphs or information on productivity
- Quality and safety standards

10 Monitor knowledge of such things as:

- Procedures
- Prospects for promotion
- Trade union elections (if recognised)
- Training facilities
- Health and safety

APPENDIX 7

TeamTalk

REPORT BACK

FROM	TO		
ITEMS DISCUSSED	QUESTIONS / SUGGESTIONS	DEALT WITH (Tick)	REFERRED UPWARDS TO
1	1		
	2		
	3		
2			
	4		
	5		
3			
	6		
	7		
4	8		
	9		
	10		

British Telecommunications
Cardiff Telephone Area

NOTES (To relate to number of question/suggestion overleaf)

1

2

3

4

5

6

7

8

9

10

MEMBERS OF TEAM NOT BRIEFED	REASON

British Telecommunications
Cardiff Telephone Area

Industrial Society services

The Industrial Society runs courses and conferences, and can offer a wide range of in-company help and advice to organisations to make Team Briefing effective.

For further information on Team Briefing contact:

The Communication Department
The Industrial Society
Robert Hyde House
48 Bryanston Square
London W1H 7LN
Telephone 01-262 2401